Dropshipping

*The Ultimate Dropshipping
BLUEPRINT Made Simple*

—

*Find, Launch, And Sell Your First
Private-Label Product*

If you're interested in learning more ways to start or expand your business, I've added a preview of another book of mine at the end of this book, about *Etsy: The Ultimate Guide Made Simple for Entrepreneurs to Start Their Handmade Business and Grow To an Etsy Empire*

Check out the whole book and other books written by me on Amazon.com.

Introduction

Have you ever thought of starting your own online business? If so, this book is for you. In this book, we discuss how to start selling products online through drop shipping.

In this method of doing business, you will be able to start selling products without the need to rent space for a storefront. In fact, the products no longer need to pass through you. It goes to the buyer straight from the distributor.

You can start this business in less than a thousand dollars. You can start with even less if you can do everything by yourself. In this book, we discuss the skills required to get this business off the ground and to make it successful. The information in this book is organized so that even beginners can start doing business.

We hope that the information in this book will help you start your own business. Begin reading this book and start increasing your income today!

Table of Contents

Chapter 1

What is a Drop Shipping Business?

Drop shipping is one of the most popular ways of starting an online business. In this type of online business, you are selling products online but the products you sell never pass through you. Instead, the products you are selling goes directly from the source to the buyer.

The manufacturer creates the product. They may either store the products themselves or send it to a distributor to be sent out to people interested in the product. In normal circumstances, retailers contact the people who store the products. They order large amounts of the product and sell the products in their own stores.

Some of these distributors find that delivering directly to products users can also be profitable. They allow buyers to call them up directly and buy products from them. You can make an agreement so that the drop shipping companies will deliver to your customers.

Now that you have access to the products and a way to deliver them, you need to find ways to let people know that you are selling these products. Using various online marketing strategies, you will be able to let people know that they can have this product delivered to their homes.

If interested people see your product marketing, they may contact you or order from your store. If they complete the online purchase, you should already have their money. You should let the drop shipping company know about the purchase. Use part of their money to pay the drop shipping company. The drop shipping company then sends the product to the buyer.

For each purchase, you earn the difference between your selling price and the fees you pay the manufacturer or the distributor. The fees usually include the price of the product and the delivery and handling fees.

The profit can be a few dollars or a few hundred dollars depending on the type of product that you are selling.

Chapter 2

Finding a Profitable Product

The first challenge that you need to face when setting your first drop shipping business is finding a product that will sell.

Steps in finding a product to sell

1. Choose a niche market

All the marketing gurus will tell you to choose an industry that you are interested in. If you like sports, for example, you should look for a sports-related product. If you like fashion, you should probably choose this industry to start your drop shipping business. Start by listing the industries for which you want to start an online store. Here are some of the most popular industries online:

- Health and Wellness

- Fitness and Outdoors

- Sports

- Hobbies and crafts

- Home and kitchen products

- Tech and gadgets

- Computers and laptops

These are only some of the most popularly searched industries online all year round. You can add other industries that you have some experience with.

If you have chosen an industry, you should look for a niche in that industry that you could start a profitable business with. If you like sports, for instance, you may start by stating the specific types of sports that you know and enjoy. You could then look for certain products related to the sport that are sold by drop shipping companies.

When choosing a niche, also consider the communities that you are already connected with. Let's say you want to sell standing basketball hoops for homeowners. This is a big-ticket item in the sports and outdoor industry. It would be easier to start makings online sales if you already know where prospective buyers of the product are hangings out online. If you are considering multiple market niches, you should choose the ones where you already have access to their communities.

2.   Find trending product types

You should find products with online marketing potential. To find products like these in your chosen niche, check for products related to your niche in popular e-commerce websites like Amazon. Nowadays, you can find all types of products in these websites.

It is not advisable to sell the same products you find on Amazon or any other e-commerce website. When people search for these products in the search engine, they are most likely to see Amazon pages on top of the search result page. It is almost impossible for you to beat Amazon pages in search result pages for specific product keywords.

Instead, you should look for popular product types and find alternative products for them that are not sold on Amazon and other e-commerce websites yet.

If you are planning to start selling your products in a specific area, you should also check if it is being sold in your local stores. If similar products are available in your local stores, check their prices. This will give you an idea of the amount of competition that your business will face.

Lastly, consider products that are not easily available to your target buyers. Let's say you want to start marketing the product to people in your town, you should consider if they have access to it in your local stores. If a certain product can be easily bought from these sources, they are more likely to choose the offline stores. They will only choose your online store if your store offers significantly lower prices than the competition.

3. Find product types that do not update often

When setting up online stores, it will be easier for you if there is little need for updates for the products. Some types of products like the ones in the tech industry upgrade often. Every time these products upgrade, you also need to do updates on your product pages. Choose products that do not have this problem.

4. Examine the demand for the product

When you have chosen the types of products that you are interested in selling, examine if people look for them often. Let's say you want to start selling specialized types of exercise bicycles. You noticed that they are not available in your city, and you found a certain brand that is not on Amazon yet.

Before you start looking for a supplier for that product, you should first check if there is a demand for it in the online market. You can check on Amazon for products similar to it. You could check for other brands of exercise bicycles available in Amazon. If many people are making reviews on these other brands, it is a good sign that there are many buyers for that particular product online.

Aside from checking other e-commerce websites, you should check the search volume for keywords related to the products. You can do this free by using online services like Google AdWords' Keyword Planner. You should only check the keywords that show intent to buy. Using these online services, you will be able to see how often people search for the product online.

5. Check the competing websites for your product

While checking the online demand for the product, look into the amount of competition that you would face when marketing your product. Use the keywords for the product in the search engine and check the top search results. The websites you see at the top are the ones that you will be competing with when marketing your products. If they are big names online, you should probably look for other keywords to compete with or look for other types of products.

Aside from looking at these websites up, also look into the ads that may show up in the search result pages. You will also be competing with these advertisers when marketing your product. If you are still considering multiple products to sell, you should choose the ones with the least amount of competition.

Selling other brands versus creating your own brand

In the drop shipping business, you have the option to sell already established brands. If discover a drop-shipped brand that is not yet offered anywhere online, you can choose to sell on your website. However, finding a brand that is not already available can be challenging. Almost all popular brands are already sold in popular e-commerce websites.

It is very challenging to sell such brands in the business-consumer (b2c) type products. You may be able to find some brands not offered in e-commerce stores in business-business (b2b) type products. Some brand of office equipment, for instance, cannot be found on Amazon. You could contact some of these brands and ask if they offer drop shipping to buyers.

Selling already established brands can be easier if the company is active in promoting their product. If you are the first to offer their product online, they may also offer special promotions for your online store. You need to find companies that are just starting out and support them by bringing attention to their product. You also offer them a way to promote and sell their products online without setting up their own websites.

On the other hand, you could also choose to set up your own product line in your chosen niche market. To do this, you need to start looking for manufacturers of your chosen product that do not put their own labels on the products they produce. If there are a lot of factories in your area, you may find some of these products in your own city.

If you do find a type of product that you want to add to your online store, you should start developing the packaging and branding of your product. You need a name and a branding design that fits your niche and the preferences of your target market.

Lastly, promote the said product in your online store using your own brand name. In this setup, you will be promoting not only your online store but also the product and the brand.

By selling your own brand, you will have more freedom in promoting your product. All your promotions will also help your brand. By putting all your efforts in your own product, the success of your business will depend solely on your efforts. Fewer factors will be out of your control.

Aside from this, you will also be able to control the quality of your product. If you find another manufacturer with better quality products, you can switch manufacturers. You will also be in charge of the packaging of your product. Research shows that packaging is an important basis that people use in judging the quality of a brand. Other new brands may not be as meticulous in the packaging design as you are. However, you will not be able to know how the packaging looks because you never get to see the product.

Aside from the creative license of creating your own brand, you will also have the freedom in pricing if your produce your own brand. If you sell other company's brands, you may be forced to sell on a fixed price to prevent price wars among other sellers. If you create your own brand, you will be able to price your products strategically. If there are no competitions, you may sell it at a high price. If there are too may competitions at the premium price, you could lower it to be more competitive.

Examples of drop shipped products:

You can easily create your own brand if you sell general products that can be produced in bulk by a manufacturer. Some of the earliest drop shipping entrepreneurs, for example, sold different paper sizes to offices around the country. They cold-called offices in the east coast of the United States to sell paper. These offices can then, order directly from their website. They took their product from the cheapest suppliers of paper across the country. These were then packed by a fulfillment service and delivered by an independent courier.

Later, other consumable products followed. Some sold exotic tea, while others sold whey protein to fitness enthusiasts. They merely repackaged these products and sold them as their own brands.

You can also start selling common consumable products repackaged as your own brands. However, you need to find the right manufacturers and distributors for them.

Characteristics of products that sell well online

Whenever people buy from companies they are not familiar with over the internet, they are risking their money. You need to choose the types of products that are worth taking the risk for.

Here are some of the reasons that people risk their money with new online stores:

- They are looking for specialized products

Some types of products just cannot be found in offline stores and e-commerce websites. This is the reason why you need to find niche markets that other online marketers are not familiar with. The types of products that you sell should solve unique types of problems.

- They need to see tutorials before buying

Some types of products also require special instructions to use. Because of this, people are forced to go online to look for tips on how to use the product. When they find the information they need in a website that also offers the product, they may buy from that website.

- Aim to be the exclusive distributor of a product online

One of the best ways to become successful in your drop shipping business is by becoming the exclusive distributor of a product in the online market. Most established brands would not give you this privilege. You are more likely to succeed in becoming an exclusive distributor of newer brands or products.

If you are confident that you can bring in solid sales numbers, you should also consider asking to be the exclusive distributor to a certain area. If your online store, for example, has a strong online presence in the east coast of the United States, you may have some negotiating leverage to ask to be the exclusive sales outlet of a brand in a certain area.

- Products cheaper than offline counterparts

Some people buy from new online stores because of the lower cost. Unlike brick and mortar stores, e-commerce websites do not have high overhead costs. They do not need to rent warehouses or storefronts to sell. Because of this, they may be able to offer lower prices of products. Because people are ordering in small quantities, however, the drop shipping system may have additional shipping and handling costs. You should sell products that offer good prices even with the shipping and handling fees considered.

Chapter 3

Getting in Touch with the Right Suppliers

After researching about the products that you may be interested in selling, you should now have a list of products that you want to sell. The next step is to look for the suppliers of these products that offer drop shipping. When looking for the suppliers of your product, you should first learn about the types of suppliers in the dropship business.

Manufacturers

If you are lucky, the manufacturer of the product that you have chosen may be offering drop-shipping services to buyers of their products. Manufacturers offer the lowest price for products. If you can make a deal with the manufacturer of the product, you will be able to offer a competitive price to your buyers.

Distributors

If the manufacturer of the product does not offer drop shipping, look for a local distributor who does. Distributors are companies that facilitate the logistics for the manufacturer. They usually own large warehouses that store certain products to be delivered to selected locations. The scope of their delivery system limits the areas where you can sell your products.

If you cannot find a manufacturer for a brand that you want to sell on your website, look for a distributor that may have it. Because these distributors need to get their piece of the pie, there will be added cost to the product. It will be hard to set a competitive price for your products if you buy from a distributor that has a big profit margin compared to the price of the manufacturer.

Finding suppliers for the products you want

If you choose to sell other people's brand, you will need to start looking up the local factories and warehouses of that brand. You can start by looking up the company's website. You should then, contact them by phone or through email.

To get the attention of the company, you need to have a business proposal prepared before meeting with representatives of the company. A company who are already drop shipping their products will compare your proposal to people whom they are already doing business with. It helps if you can convince them that you will be able to sell your products through your personal connections and through online marketing.

Companies will be more interested in how you will promote their products and how this can lead to more sales. You should use all the tricks that you will learn later in the book in your business proposal to these suppliers.

Using the internet to find untapped goldmines

When looking for the best suppliers, you need to take a lot of time website hopping. When looking for wholesalers on the internet, you should consider that the companies that you are looking for are not skilled in online marketing. That's why they need your help to move the products.

You may encounter a website that looks like it was created in 1999. You should not dismiss companies just by the look of their website. Contact all possible leads for products that will give you a competitive edge in the market.

Be careful with drop-shipping services specially set up for online marketers. You will encounter some websites that offer you many products. They may make the process easy for you to start. They may have some offers that seem too good to be true like having no minimum order limits or having very low fees.

Scrutinize these companies before applying for their business. Even if they are legitimate companies, they may be offering the products to many other online marketers. You will need to compete with these people when promoting the product. You may end up with a price war if the prices of the products are not regulated.

When looking for suppliers of the product, you should also consider narrowing the location down to the target of your marketing. Let's say you want to start selling a special brand of tea in New Mexico. You chose the state because that particular brand of tea is not yet available there. If you are looking for drop-shippers for the tea, you should limit your search to companies that send directly to New Mexico. You could specify this in your search.

You should also consider the products produced in your own city. This way, you will be able to keep in touch with the company. If you can meet with the supplier in person, you may be able to get deals that other marketers cannot get.

Considering supplier requirements

For brands that are already drop shipping their products, you only need to comply with their partnership requirements. In most cases, you will be required to apply for a wholesale account by a manufacturer or a distributor. They will check if you are capable of moving large amounts of products with your business model. If they see that your business is capable, you will be approved.

In this part of the process, you should be mindful of the fees that the drop-shippers will require. They will charge a small fee per order. The amount can go for $2-$7 per shipping. The prices vary depending on the weight, size and shape of the product being shipped. You need to consider this fee when pricing your products.

You should also think about the minimum order sizes. Some wholesale distributors and product manufacturers do not allow small orders. They want to minimize the cost of logistics by requiring a minimum order from sellers.

In this case, you will need to take the cost of the minimum order into consideration. Most companies will allow you to pay the cost of the minimum order ahead of time. This will give the suppliers security that you will be in business with them for a while.

Having products specially made for you

If you are planning to create your own brand, on the other hand, you may need to have products made according to your specifications. You need to have constant communication with the manufacturer of the products to pull this off.

You should be communicating with the manufacturers so that you will be able to check the quality of the products. You will also be taking charge of the packaging of the product so that it fits the branding and marketing plan you have set.

When looking for companies to make products for you, you should look into manufacturers that produce certain types of products without putting their own branding into it. A bakeshop that specializes in making cookies, for example, may choose not to sell directly to consumers. Instead, they sell their products to bakeries and coffee shops. In the process, they also add packaging according to the company ordering a product from them.

You could also do the same. You will find these types of manufacturers in local factories. You should look into the types of products being produced around your area. You could also widen your search if you cannot find these types of manufacturers. You should also take advantage of local business directories to find a contact number of companies who offer this kind of services. You should make use of directories from current sources like trade magazines and websites.

Some companies may ask for a fee for access to their directories. You should only use these services if you trust the source of these directories. You should not join groups that require recurring membership fees. You only need the information for a short period making membership unnecessary after the research period.

Aside from trade magazines, you should also hunt for trade shows around your state for the niche market that you want to start a business with. You will be able to find companies that are unknown to consumers in these events. Some of them may offer specialized manufacturing, packaging and drop shipping of the product you want.

Some of these companies may have some online presence, but you may need to search extensively to find them. As mentioned earlier, these companies do not spend a lot on online marketing. They may only be maintaining a website in case some of their clients look them up.

Drawbacks of having products manufactured for you

Though making your own brand may sound exciting, it is extremely challenging to start from nothing. Because people have not heard of your brand yet, you should expect that it would take some time for sales to pick-up. Because your product is new, you may need to compete aggressively with other brands in the market. In most cases, your biggest advantage is the lower price of your product. You need to consider this when you are just entering the market.

It will also be difficult to find manufacturers who also do packaging and drop shipping. In most cases, you will need to have the products manufactured in one company and then packaged and shipped in another. The additional steps in the logistics will add to the price of the product.

The advantage to this is that you will be able to choose the packaging and courier companies that offer the lowest price.

Advantages of creating your own brand

If you do choose to create your own brand, you will have complete marketing freedom when promoting your product. You will also be able to add value to your products through additional items. You can add additional products in the packaging for loyal customers. You will also be able to create your own special promotions.

When you are selling other people's brands, you are sharing promotions with other marketers. When the brand you are selling has a discount for the day, all other marketers also get to use the same promotion. You can only get specialized promotions if you create exclusive deals with the company.

If you create your own brands, you will be able to create your own promotions. You can time your promotions to compete with other product promotions in the market.

Setting up the Products

Before you start selling, you should first make sure that you have all factors considered about the product.

The price

For each product you put up in your store, make sure that the price is competitive compared to competing products in the market. First, consider the competing products available in brick and mortar stores.

If the type of product you are offering is available in stores, people are less likely to go online to buy them. The only exception is when the offline varieties are too expensive. You should be able to offer the products at discounted rates even when considering shipping and handling fees.

Compare the product price to competing products in the online market. If the product you are selling is also available on Amazon and other popular e-commerce websites, you will find it difficult competing with the online marketing of these companies. The best way to beat these stores is by setting a competitive price.

Most manufacturers will give you the product at low prices. It's usually the shipping and handling fees that increase the prices. To lower the cost of this part of the business, consider choosing to put most of your marketing efforts to the most logistically strategic areas for your manufacturer or your distributor. If your manufacturer is located on the east coast, for example, your marketing efforts should target the east coast area.

If most of your sales come from the other side of the country, you should find manufacturers or distributors in that part of the country.

Packaging and branding

If you are selling your own product, you also need to take care of the packaging of your products. You need to make sure that they packaging will be strong to endure the handling on the road. While considering this, you also need to consider the appearance of the logo, color scheme and the arrangement of the product inside the box or the container.

If you can meet with the packaging people, you need to specify how you want your product to look inside the box. To check the toughness of your product packaging, you could order your own product and check its arrangement and overall appearance once it arrives.

Chapter 4

Creating your Online Store and your Business Processes

Now that you have your products, you need to start building your marketing tools. In place of a store, you will have a website where people can complete their transactions. In this website, you need the following features:

A product list page

In this page, you need to include a list of the products. Each product included in this list should contain a photo, price, and the product name. Most people who reach your websites are not ready to buy yet. Instead, they will look around. The goal of this page is to make people click on the individual products. This will lead them to the product page.

A page for each product

In this page, people should see the description of a particular product. You should include high-quality photos of the product from all angles in this page. You should also include the specs of the product to inform the prospect buyers what the product has to offer.

It is also important to have a user generated review system on this page. People are used to seeing these user reviews in popular e-commerce websites – and they like those for good reason. It gives credibility to your products as it enables them to make better buying decisions. Without it, it is unlikely that your visitors will buy from you.

The goal of this page is to make people click on the 'call to action' button. There should always be one visible in the page. You can add an 'add this to my shopping cart' button next to the product and at the bottom of the page. You should adjust the words, color, shape, size and location of the button to try to increase the conversion rate of the page.

A checkout page

When people click on the 'call to action' button in the product page, they should be led to the shopping cart. This is the start of the checkout process. If the visitor is satisfied with the price and the specs of the product, they may proceed and add their credit card information or pay via PayPal.

These are the most important pages in an online website. You may add more pages depending on the type of marketing strategies that you want to run.

After preparing the basic parts of the website, you should also start setting up your business process. More specifically, you need to create a list of tasks that you need to do once you receive an order. Here are some of the basic tasks:

1. Wait for orders to reach the minimum shipping limit of the company.

2. Once the minimum amount of orders has been reached, you should send the details to the fulfillment company.

3. Pay the company their share and leave the proceeds in your own account

You also need to consider the customer service process. Ideally, you should have a contact number or email address in the packaging of your product so that buyers can contact you afterwards. You should state a time for accepting complaints about orders.

The most efficient way to set up your customer service hotline is by outsourcing the process to an off shore virtual assistant. It will cost you a few dollars an hour, but you will be able to free up some time.

If you are just starting out, you need to start with just email support. With email support, you can entertain customer services questions and complaints by yourself. You no longer need to hire another employee. You need to set a time in each day to check the complaints. In the beginning, there will be few complaints. As long as your marketing strategies do not lie about your product, you will not get irate customers. However, as the range of your sales widen all over the country, the number of complaint emails will also rise.

The best strategy when dealing with this is by taking note of all the complaints from the customers. You should then, create a standard systematic plan on how to deal with these common complaints.

Chapter 5

Your Product Launch Checklist

Now that you have the product set, you need to set and prepare for the launching of the product. On your launch date, you need to take as much attention as you can in your target location of business. Before you launch your business, you should consult this checklist:

- ✓ Business license and tax considerations
- ✓ Approval from the FDA for ingested products
- ✓ Contract with the manufacturer, distributor or both
- ✓ Supply chain description
- ✓ Packaging and branding of the product
- ✓ Delivery testing
- ✓ Website pages, functions and payment security
- ✓ Order fulfillment process
- ✓ Selling in other e-commerce websites
- ✓ Marketing plan

We will discuss the marketing plan in later parts of the book. You need to keep this list handy when you are thinking about launching your business.

Chapter 6

Getting Product Reviews

As stated earlier in the book, people will trust your product and your company more if you put up user reviews on the product page. However, it will be hard getting reviews in the beginning when no one has bought the product yet.

- Ask reviews in your launch event

To start getting product reviews, you need to attract people who are interested in getting your product free or at a discount. If you plan to start your marketing process in your town, for example, you can start asking for reviews from the people you know.

In your product or company launch party, you could start giving products away free in contests or other types of activities with prices. You could also start selling the product at the party. If the people in your launch party are having a good time, they may buy the product as a way to thank you.

In the same event, you should request the people who just got the product to give a review on the company website. If you are also selling your personal brand in other e-commerce websites, you should be mindful of the transparency rules of the website. The reviewers should state if they received the product free or if they were given a discount in exchange for the review.

- Ask your family and friends

You should also encourage your family and friends to leave their own reviews on the website. You could have them try the product and encourage them to say something about it on the website. If they like you, they are likely to give your product a positive review.

- Encourage buyers to review your product

If you are confident that your product will satisfy most buyers, you should put a personal letter in with the product addressed to the buyer. In the letter, you should thank them for the purchase and ask them if they can leave a review if they are satisfied with the product. In case they are not satisfied, you can ask them to email your customer support hotline.

The letter addressed to the buyer will encourage them to go back to your website and leave a review.

- Encourage reviews in your customer service hotline

You could also encourage people who contact your customer service number or email to leave a product review. To avoid negative reviews, though, you should only encourage the ones who are satisfied with your service and your product. You could ask them to leave a review after you've resolved their problems.

- Dealing with negative reviews

Most people with the intent to buy your product want to see the negative reviews about it. If they can live with these negative reviews, they will still buy the product. However, if the negative reviews are deal breakers, you should take action starting with your own evaluation of the impact, the product, and the brand/supplier.

- Avoid negative reviews altogether

The best way to deal with negative reviews is to avoid them altogether. You will be able to avoid this by making sure that your product and brand promotions are not promising something that your product does not provide. The buyers should get what they state in the ad copies.

You could also avoid negative reviews if you have an active customer service presence. Customer service is even more important if the product you are offering requires assembly or needs the buyer to follow complicated instructions. For products like these, you should expect to receive about instructions in your customer service communications.

Lastly, one of the best ways to avoid negative reviews is by having a money-back guarantee. The 'money-back' guarantee is an effective pre-sale and post-sale marketing tool. People who are still doubtful about your product will still buy it thinking that they can still return it if they do not like it. After the purchase, they will not complain as violently if they have the option to return it.

- Reply to negative reviews

People who are used to buying things online often see products with no negative reviews as suspicious. You should not delete the negative reviews in your product pages. Instead, you should show that you try to deal with all the complaints by posting a reply to all negative reviews.

These replies should not sound defensive. Instead, you should apologize for the inconvenience to the buyer and ask for their email address so that you can address their complaints. Your replies should also show that you aim to help them solve their problems.

By leaving a message in all negative reviews, you are showing the presence of your customer service staff. Most companies no longer maintain post-purchase communication with buyers. Frequent online buyers know that a good customer service is rare in the online shopping world. If you show that you give customer service, the buyers will not be afraid to buy from you.

- Creating changes to deal with common complaints

After selling the first batch of the product, you should communicate with the manufacturer of the products and tell them about the common complaints that it gets. Some of the common problems can be taken care of in the manufacturing stage.

Some of the common complaints will come from the packaging and fulfillment stage. You should also communicate with the people who are in charge of these stages to make sure that the problems will not return in future orders.

- Changing brand or model names

If a product has received too many complaints or if requires too many changes, you may be able to start with a clean slate if you just create a new brand name or model name for that product. With a major change in the appearance and the name of the product, the market may not associate the new changes to the old product. The bad reputation of the old product will not transfer to the new one.

The only drawback of changing these factors is that you need to start anew with the promotion and the marketing of the product. All the resources that have gone to marketing the old product will be wiped out, and the popularity of the old product will not transfer to the new one.

Chapter 7

Creating Great Impact during Product Launch

Introducing your product to your target market is probably the most important step in the marketing stage of the product. In this stage, you are trying to let as many people as possible know about your product in the shortest time to increase sales.

1. Creating a launch campaign

You should consider your product or company launch as a giant marketing campaign to reach as many buyers as possible. You need to combine both online and offline marketing to let the people know about the brand and the product. You should also take this opportunity to show your advantages compared to competing brands and products.

2. Choose a launch date

Choosing a launch date is important in a drop shipping business. When choosing your launch date, you could choose from these different strategies:

- Launch at a high online traffic season

You can choose to launch your website on a high traffic season. If you have a high budget for your launch date marketing, you should schedule your launch date before the holidays or during the post-thanksgiving online sale. During these days, there are many people buying stuff online. Some of them are buying for themselves with their holiday money, but most of them are buying gifts for their loved ones.

You will receive a lot of traffic in these times if your product does not have a lot of competition online. To take advantage of the flood of online shoppers in these days, you should start advertising and promoting your products 4-6 weeks before the holiday.

You will need a big budget when promoting your products in these seasons because you will be competing with major brands. Most online e-commerce websites will also be pushing their products online at these seasons. You should compete with their advertising bids. You may also see higher advertising fees from private websites when in these specific days.

However, if you can roll with the punches when competing with these websites, you will be able to get more traffic and more sales. It all comes down to your marketing budget. If you can afford it and if your profit margin will allow it, you should compete with the big boys in these seasons.

- Launch in a season specifically for your product

If you do not have enough money for promoting your products in the peak seasons of online sales, you could also choose a launch date before a major season for your niche. If you sell football training equipment or example, you can start selling your products around the Super Bowl seasons. In these times, people a going online to look up the schedule of the game and for discounted tickets. You could take advantage of the increased online traffic in your niche. Some of these people want to train their kids in the sport. You can target your marketing efforts to target these people specifically.

If you are selling health and fitness products, on the other hand, you can put your launching date right after the holiday break. People usually pig out on holiday food. In an effort to make their health-related New Year's resolution a reality, they will look for products that can help them. You should take advantage of that by putting your launch date around these days.

After choosing your launch date, you should start thinking about your product launching marketing campaign.

3. Offline marketing

Before you start your online marketing, you should first set the locations where you want to get your buyers. Most drop shipping entrepreneurs dream of spreading their product all over the country. However, the reach of your business will be severely limited by the reach of your distributors. Sometimes, it will cost too much for buyers to have the product shipped from the other side of the country.

If you have chosen the location where you will start your marketing campaign, you should look for low-cost marketing opportunities that will let the people know about your product. One way to do this is by selling your product in local stores. This may not be the ideal drop shipping practice, but it gets the products moving. Contact local business through phone if they are interested in selling your products in their store. If they are interested, you can give them a discount while still making a profit. You should then direct them to your website where they can order the product.

Aside from local businesses, you should also try to reach special groups that may be interested in using your product. If you are selling special sports training equipment, for example, you can contact coaches in local schools if they are interested in trying your equipment out.

Take advantage of business-to-consumer trade shows. These tradeshows receive a lot of traffic. You will be able to get a lot of attention to your unique products in these events.

You should also find ways to get your product in media outlets that your target market is interacting with. If your research shows that your target buyers listen to the radio, you can sponsor songs or radio shows in these radio stations.

4. Online Marketing

You should also put a lot of effort in online marketing during your launch date. You should let people know that your website is ready for business on the launch date. You should also let it run a few days or weeks before your launch date. This will make interested buyers become

Prior to the launch date, you should already create social media accounts and post content about your launch date. For example, you could do a countdown of the days before your launch date.

You should also include a link to a landing page where people can read about the company and when they can start ordering products. You could also add an email capturing field where people can start subscribing to news about the company and the launch event.

Aside from these types of product and company promotions, you should also start doing paid promotions. You can put up ads in Google AdWords for people using your target keywords. You should also include ads in social networks where your target market may be spending a lot of their time.

If there are information websites where most of your prospect buyers go, you could contact the owners of those websites to start a traffic sharing agreement. Because your website does not have a lot of traffic yet, you need to pay them to share some of their traffic. They will be happy to put up links to your website for a price.

You can learn to use these paid advertising channels if you give it some time. However, if you do not want to do that, you may also choose to pay professionals to it for you. By choosing to let professionals do it, you will be able to optimize your online campaign. They will create all your ad copies to catch people's attention. By paying an extra amount, you will be able to maximize the reach and effectiveness of your advertising campaign. If you do not have time to learn how to advertise online before your launching, you could use the services of these companies.

All these marketing activities should be done in 1-2 weeks of your launch date. Your goal is to let prospect buyers know about your product from all type of media.

5. Create a product launching event

You should celebrate your product launching with an event in a place where most of your prospect buyers can go. The event can be a simple marketing campaign to let people know that your product exists. You may put up a booth in a local mall in the city where you will be marketing your product. You could also start an online contest and advertise it in social networks and in search engines.

In these events, you should create a reason for people to go to your online store and buy a product. For instance, you could give them a coupon that they can use to get the products at a discount. The coupon should have a time limit so that there will be some sense of urgency in the people who are interested in buying.

Chapter 8

Setting Up Your Long-term Promotion Plan

While launching your product is designed to increase sales in the first days of your business, you also need to create a long-term marketing plan. In this plan, you should create marketing campaigns to keep increasing the number of sales. Your sales performance should keep increasing every campaign period. You can compare your current sales performance from the previous months. If it declined, you should find out the reason for that. You continue to try to beat your best sales performance by improving your marketing campaigns.

Social media marketing

To keep your product relevant you should engage in long-term social media marketing. Business-to-consumer types of products do well in image-centered social networks like Instagram, Pinterest, and Facebook. Business-to-business types, on the other hand, should be marketed in social networks for professionals like LinkedIn and Twitter.

All you have to do to succeed in promoting your products in these marketing channels is to keep being active. This means that you need to keep posting content on your social network accounts. The content that you share should be connected with your products. You should also consider your audience when choosing this content.

Luckily, for you, you already have many business pages to copy from. You should check the Facebook accounts of your competitors to learn what they are posting. More importantly, you need to learn how they attract engagement from their audience and how they send their audience to their websites.

If you have a virtual assistant, social media posting is one of the tasks that you can delegate to them. You can have them research the best posts to add to the account. You will know if they are good at it by checking the amount of engagement that they get.

Aside from posting regularly, you should also choose the timing of your posts. You should choose to post in times when your target audience are online and using the social networks. Most people use social networks for example on their commute to work. You can add post your content at these times. Some professionals also check their social networks only in the evening, after the working day.

Aside from posting relevant content, you should also reply on possible comments of your audience. In particular, you should entertain comments that ask about the product. These comments may lead to a sale. If you state that your page is about a product or a business, Facebook adds a reviews section in your page. You should also keep track of the reviews that you get in this area of your page.

When people check your online presence, they will check if your company responds to comments. If they see that you are active in replying to complaints, this may convince them to buy your product.

Most importantly, you should also add well-spaced 'call to action' posts. These posts directly promote your product or send your social media audience to your website. 5-10% of your total posts should contain a 'call to action' to go to the website or buy a product. Posting too many promotional posts will drive some people away from your social media accounts. People who think that you only post promotional content will unfollow your page. Some will just ignore your posts. This will decrease the engagement in your posts. If there are few engagements in your posts, they are less likely to reach the feeds of other users.

You should achieve balance to keep people engaged in your page while still driving people to your business. Let's say you post in your Facebook account 5 times a day. In the first three days of the week, you should only post entertaining and informational content. On the fourth day, you can post 1/5 promotional content.

Search engine optimization

You should also use search engine optimization to start attracting people from the search engine. Unfortunately, only the most popular e-commerce websites rank well in the search engines. If you want to improve your ranking in search engines, you need to create other parts of the site.

Aside from the e-commerce section of your website, you can also add a company blog where you post content related to your product. If the product is complicated, for instance, you can post how-to instructions to guide buyers. It will also show your prospect buyers that there are documentations that they can turn to help them after they purchase the items.

Posting in a blog regularly will increase your search page presence on your selected page. You can also post your blog posts in your social networking accounts to drive more traffic to your website.

Aside from posting regular content, you should also start optimizing each page and post in your website for the search engine crawler bots. Search engines try to map out the net by using crawler bots to visit websites, categorize them and follow links. You should make your website pages and posts easy to crawl and categorize.

In both your e-commerce store and your blog, you should include your target search keywords in the H1 and H2 attributes. These parts of a webpage indicate the title of the page. These attributes tell the search engine what the page is about. If possible, you should also add the relevant keywords to your page in the first paragraph of your content.

You should also add more than 400 words per page. Even your product pages should contain more than 400 words. Pages with words less than this amount generally do not rank well. You should also add photos relevant to your content. You should then include your target keyword in the alt-attribute of these images.

Links are probably the most important ranking factor in search engine marketing. In recent years, however, Google search algorithms have become stricter and smarter in judging websites based on their links. You should only get high-quality links that point to your websites. You can do this by commissioning outsourced employees to write guest posts on other popular blogs and websites in your niche. You should only instruct them to post links in websites that are popular in the niche market.

Avoid 'black hat' link building techniques because Google penalizes websites with too many links from bad quality websites. If you do not have the time to do all these tasks, you can pay professional search engine and social media marketers to do these tasks for you. You can tell them your goals, and they will try to use the best strategies to attract traffic and convert them into customers.

Paid promotional activities

You should also put some effort in paid promotions. These methods should create both short-term and long-term marketing results. Before you execute the specific promotional activities, however, you first need to create your landing page.

Create your landing page

All your online promotions lead to your landing page. This page contains a marketing copy that convinces people to buy your product. This page should be hosted on your website, but it should not contain too many distractions. There should not be links to other parts of the website like menus and content suggestions. It should only contain one link. This link should lead to the shopping cart and later to the checkout page.

- Affiliate marketing

You should also take advantage of the large number of entrepreneurs who are trying to earn money online. One of the best ways to earn money online is through affiliate marketing. In this process, other people with good online presence talk about your product and promote it to their audience. In the process, they post affiliate links that you give them.

The traffic from these affiliate links are tracked on your website. If the traffic from these links leads to a sale, the person who promoted your product for you gets a percentage of the sale.

To create your own affiliate marketing campaign, you should start by contacting some of the most popular affiliate marketing companies online like Rakuten LinkShare and Commission Junction. They will help you develop your first affiliate marketing campaign. More importantly, they have a good number of publishers who are ready to promote your product for you.

To become a successful affiliate marketer, you need to achieve a balance between the commission rate that you give out and the amount of profit that you get from a sale. If you post higher commission rates, more people will promote your product. However, as you increase your commission rates, your overall profit per sale also decreases.

- Online advertising

As discussed earlier in the book, there are many different ways to advertise online. In general, online advertising is cheaper, and its results are easily measurable compared to offline promotions.

The easiest way to advertise online is through advertising networks of big companies like Google and Bing. These websites post your ads on search result pages and on their partner websites. They charge per click in your ad. You only pay if people click on your ad.

- Online events

Aside from promoting your products the traditional way, you should also do events that will drive people to your website. In these events, you should give away your own products as prizes. You will get positive reviews from people who win these events.

If you are selling consumable items, you can make the contests exclusive to people who already own your products. By doing this, you will encourage these people to become loyal to your products. They are also more likely to return to your website in the future if you have contests or other promotional events.

Chapter 9

Avoiding Common Drop Shipping Pitfalls

Drop shipping is an easy and low-cost way of starting a profitable company. However, you should not expect it to be a cakewalk. You will experience some challenges. These challenges affect your sales numbers. Most people who fail in drop shipping site these challenges as the major reasons. Here are some of them:

1. Subpar shipping and handling time

The biggest e-commerce websites like Amazon have developed an efficient system of fulfilling orders. Because your manufacturer or distributor does not have as many facilities as these companies, they may not be able to deliver goods as fast.

You should only use the manufacturers' drop shipping service for locations near the company. As a solution for long shipping times in other parts of the country, you could also sell your brand on Amazon and use Fulfillment by Amazon to deliver in far parts of the country. You should then have the manufacturer send the product to the nearest Amazon fulfillment center.

2. Brand development takes a long time

You should also consider the amount of time it takes to build a brand. The most popular brands in your niche may have taken decades to become big. Be ready for the long haul.

To hasten your brand development, you should always be aggressive in your marketing efforts. If you have a low marketing budget, you should consider focusing your paid promotions to a small area. If you are just starting out or example, you could focus your ads and free online campaign in the nearest big city to your source of products. In the beginning, the people you sell to will be satisfied by the shipping time and may order again in the future.

3. Orders may arrive below the standard expected by the customers

Because you are just drop shipping your products without ever seeing them, some of the products may not be as well arranged as the ones in the advertisement images. Some drop shipping entrepreneurs become frustrated when this happens because they have very little control of the appearance of the product they are selling.

To avoid this, you should start with manufacturers who are near your home. This way, you will be able to talk with the manufacturing or packaging manager on how to improve the appearance of the product when it arrives.

In some cases, you may need to hire a different packaging company to make sure that your instructions will be applied. Before you set up your business, you should also discuss the return and refund policies of the company. Your online store will become more successful if it has a return policy. However, not all manufacturers allow returns. Those who do allow them also have specific guidelines on how it should be done. Be aware of these guidelines so that you will be able to protect the rights of your buyers and the integrity of your brand.

4. Avoid overpriced products

In some cases, sales may not go up because of the high price of the product. Shopping for drop shipped products is generally more expensive than buying offline. You can still get many sales even with a high price if you choose specialized products that are not easily found in malls and in big e-commerce websites. You should also set the anchor price by comparing the price of your product to other high-priced brands

5. Bad business partners

After signing up with the vendor of the product, you may find some of their business practices unappealing. Some of them may take too long to send the product. Others may use low-quality materials in the manufacturing.

Always be in the lookout for other manufacturer or distributors of your products. Look for other companies that may replace your current business partners in case the latter does not deliver on their end of the business.

Conclusion

I hope this book had given you all the information you need to start your drop shipping business.

The next step is to start looking for an industry that you want to work for. It is important that you are passionate about that industry to make sure that you do not lose interest in the future. Online marketing is an enjoyable way of doing business if you love the industry that you are working for.

You should then, go back to the chapters in this book to start developing a business plan to convince manufacturers to do business with you.

Finally, if you enjoyed this book, then I'd like to ask you for a favor, would you be kind enough to leave an honest review for this book on Amazon? It would help people who are looking for the same information as you to know if this is a book for them or not, and it would be **greatly appreciated!**

Go to Amazon.com to leave a review for this book!

Thank you and good luck,
Michelle Williams

Preview of *Etsy*: *The Ultimate Guide Made Simple for Entrepreneurs to Start Their Handmade Business and Grow To an Etsy Empire*

Introduction

Do you like making handmade items that reflect your artistic, whimsical, or romantic side? Or perhaps, you just love going antiquing and raiding your grandparent's old trunk and cupboards? Then Etsy should be the place for you.

For a long time now, Etsy has become the go-to online marketplace for artisans who want to get their pieces out into the market or for hobbyists who want to earn a little extra. And if you have a great product, some business savvy, and good marketing intuition, then you're sure to find a niche in Etsy.

The competition is tough, but this book is going to help you gain success on Etsy. Here, you'll find all the basic information you need to start your own shop, create a strong brand, and catch shoppers' attention. You will find tips on how to make the best of your item listings, descriptions, and titles, as well as how to take great pictures that really show off your items.

Having trouble with the math? Don't worry! This book also has that covered. You will find simple and easy guides that will help you get the right price and ensure that you get the profits you deserve!

Go through this book and create your own Etsy empire!

Chapter 1:
All About Etsy

For everyone who has a love of handmade, original, and vintage crafts, Etsy is certainly the place to be. It is the biggest and most popular place to buy and sell handmade crafts and supplies, giving creators, artists, and entrepreneurs a place to start off their businesses with little hassle and a big marketplace. In Etsy, There are plenty of opportunities for anyone who wants to start a small business.

The Etsy Business Model

In order for you to fully grasp what Etsy and how you can make a living off of Etsy, you also need to understand what Etsy's business model is and how it makes money.

First of all, Etsy is not the same as eBay, although there are similar concepts. People tend to equate the two because a lot of people make many of their purchases from both sites, but there are fundamental differences.

Anything goes on eBay, but Etsy tends to have certain rules. All in all, Etsy claims that it aims to allow sellers and buyers to get reconnected with each other and give people a venue to buy and support independent artists, and small business entrepreneurs.

So how does Etsy make money? Etsy charges sellers a small fee for each item they display on the site, and they also collect a commission for every item sold, all of which are assessed at the end of the month. These fees can be paid for through a credit card or through a PayPal account.

Navigating Etsy

Registration

Anyone can look around the Etsy site and see the listed crafts on the site, but if you're intent on buying or becoming part of the Etsy community, you will have to register. Registration is free and easy and no more complicated than most other sites. All they ask for is an E-mail address, user name and password. They don't even ask for a credit card number at this point.

But if you intend to put up your craft on sale, you will need to upgrade to a seller account. This will require a major credit card such as Visa, MasterCard, or American Express, as well as your shipping and billing address.

Once you've created an account, Etsy will send you a confirmation e-mail. Make sure to check your junk and spam folder if it doesn't show up in your inbox. Once you click the link, Etsy will send you a second email welcoming you to the site.

Tips:

- Don't disregard the importance of the user name and password. Keep in mind that your user name ends up being your shop name as well and the only way you can change your shop name is by making another account. This means having to move all your items manually and having to pay another set of fees, not to mention losing the brand recognition you've been working hard to achieve. Worst of all is that you lose track of all the conversations, customer feedback, and sales records you had in the previous shop as these can't be moved to the new one, so it's probably best if you start with a really well thought out user name.

- Make sure that your password is at least 6-8 characters long and try to add some numbers and symbols in there. Don't use birthdays or anything personal that someone can easily look up. Instead, use something creative and meaningful to you alone.

- Etsy won't allow the use of profane or racist words in the username so don't even think about it! And just to be safe, don't use any trademarked words in your username.

Through the website

The homepage of any site is often where you'll find yourself returning to again and again, which is why it's important for you to understand what features Etsy's homepage offers.

The homepage gives you easy access to the numerous on-site features such as Links, Categories, Handpicked Items, Ways to Shop, Etsy Finds, Featured Seller, Blog posts and Recently listed Items.

Keep in mind that there will be fewer selections if you aren't signed in.

- The links featured at the top of the homepage make the Etsy site easy to navigate. The links let you shop, sell, gain access to community activities and the Etsy blog, also called Storque, with great posts about all things handmade. You will also find the 'Help' button among the links. If you are signed up to your account, you will also find the link to access your account, or sign out.

- Buyers have a lot of features available to them, such as the Pounce tool which lets a buyer see the listings of undiscovered sellers and the Time machine page, which allows buyers to see newly listed items, those that are expiring, and those that have been sold recently.

- The header bar gives you access to your feed, conversations, favorites and, of course, your shop. This is where the Etsy logo is, which brings you back to the homepage wherever you may be in the site, as well as links for registration and signing in (if you haven't yet). From the header bar, you can also find the links for Handmade and Vintage Items listed on the site, as well as craft supplies and other shops.

- To help buyers browse through the millions of items listed on Etsy, categories are listed. In fact, the items on sale are organized into 31 categories, such as accessories, clothing, bags, wood work, etc.

- The handpicked items featured on Etsy's homepage features items that other Etsy users have placed in the treasury list, which were then picked up by Etsy staffers and . These are often chosen according to a certain theme such as color, design, or a special holiday and can change frequently.

Tip: A good way to learn more about how others became successful on Etsy is reading up on the Featured Seller that Etsy features every few days.

Your Account

Your account gives you access to all the info you might need. It lets you keep track of your purchases, see the feedback you get from costumers, your profile, your Etsy bill, your billing and shipping info, and any apps you might be using that are related to Etsy.

Your account also has links that are very useful for new sellers, such as the Seller Handbook that has all the articles you need to know about selling on Etsy. Here, you will also find the App gallery, which features Etsy related apps that can help you manage your store, as well as all the necessary links to manage your online shop, such as your listings, options for deleting or renewing items on sale, and rearranging featured listings.

Etsy's Popularity

One of the best ways to become a good seller is by figuring out the buyer and knowing why people like shopping at Etsy.com so much.

- One of the things that shoppers love about Etsy is how easy it is for them to find, unique and high-quality items. There are thousands of handcrafted and vintage items listed on Etsy that can't be found anywhere else.

- The sheer extent of items listed on Etsy already means you're pretty sure to find what you're looking for. They have accessories, woodworks, ceramics, jewelry, metal craft and so much more. There's so much to choose from.

- It's the place to be if you're looking for craft supplies. The supplies category on Etsy already has close to a million items, ranging from fabrics to stamps, from beads to buttons.

- There are also those who, aside from enjoying the shopping experience they have at Etsy, like the fact that they are handing their money directly to the artists. This means that every purchase actually heads straight to the maker without any middlemen, which also means the items are often priced very reasonably.

All in all, the Etsy admin has done their best to make it easy to navigate the website and set up shop. If worse comes to worse, you can always ask for help from staffers if you need it, just make sure that you understand the terms and policies.

Chapter 2

Your Product

If you want to start an online business through Etsy, there are a lot of considerations. One of the most important factors are the products you will be selling after all those are what you're whole business is based on? Whether you're a professional craftsman looking to earn extra or if you're a stay at home parent aiming to turn your hobby into a small business, you have to make sure that what you're creating is something you're proud to sell.

Developing your Product Brand

There are millions of online shoppers in Etsy, just as there are millions of items listed on the site, which means you need to find a way to catch shoppers' attention and make them want to buy your product. You have to make your items stand out

Making it special

As mentioned above, one of the reasons why Etsy is so popular is because the products are often one of a kind and hold special meaning to the buyer. Successful artisans are often the ones who create items that hold deeper meaning and make buyers think, or the designs and items trigger nostalgia, romance or positive emotions. These items often have motivational, inspirational, or spiritual messages or have symbols, figures, or taglines derived from pop culture which makes them special or personal to the buyer. Having a product that speaks to many people or is "relatable" is a big leg-up for any aspiring online entrepreneur.

Tip: Spy on the competition. One of the best ways to get some great insight on the market and how to present your brand is by taking a look at some of the more successful sellers. Take a look at their products and try to see what makes it special and why many people are buying. If you happen to fall in the same category, try to take a

45

look at what makes your product different from theirs and what other feature you can add to make your product pop.

Showcasing your prime product

Choosing a prime product is important because it sets the mood for your whole store. This product should be your favorite to do as well as your favorite finished product and should be something that embodies the core of your business. You have to choose the best that you can make and build your business around it. Of course, as you grow, learn, and experiment as an artist, your business will grow and evolve too, and you can always change your prime product when you feel that your art and your business have evolved.

Getting the sales going

A little is good, but more is better

To be able to live on your online business, you will need to have consistent sales, and this means having a lot of products on your listings. A lot of Etsy sellers will tell you that business grows as you expand your listing, and most have found that there is a significant increase in sales once you reach 120 items listed on the site.

Having more products means more options for buyers, more tags, more traffic and more sales. You will have some regular shoppers who will make up a bulk of what your online transactions amount to, but new products will also attract new shoppers. Remember to stay in a certain set of categories that are connected with each other, such as shoes, clothing, bags, and accessories. Having a seemingly random listing will confuse shoppers and might put them off, for example, if you're known for selling vintage clothing, suddenly selling antique woks might not be a good idea.

Make them Match

Making products that come as a set or match together is a great idea. Making coordinated items that look great together is like inviting your customers to buy more than one item or encouraging them to come back for more once they receive the item and love the quality.

Also, you can offer discounts for customers buying sets or collections, especially if you find some of your products are starting to gather dust.

Staying ahead

There are so many online trends nowadays that just take off out of nowhere. Overnight successes aren't new and they happen almost every day. If you want to be a successful Etsy seller, you have to keep an eye out on the trends, Keep an eye on top selling products on the Etsy homepage and change or adapt according to what you think is popular. The blog page linked on Etsy's homepage can also give you some insight on which colors, styles, and gift ideas are most popular. The trending page will show which designs and patterns are currently selling and is also worth checking out.

Also, keep an eye on YOUR top selling items. If you find that a certain item is selling better, then you can think of ways to expand that line. For example, if your handcrafted sea-shell bracelets are doing well, then maybe you can add sea-shell necklaces or rings as well, or if your pink handcrafted wallets are doing well, then think of expanding in different colors. Remember that the more options you provide, the more sales you're likely to make.

Do your homework: market research

Creating products that you love is a blessing unto itself, but making a living off of it involves a bit more. You need intuition and good sense if you hope to make good money in online sales, which is why it is so important that you know your target demographic and what they really want. You have to turn the product that you love creating into something that people will love to buy as well.

You can use social media sites such as Facebook, Twitter, and Pinterest for your new products. You can post pictures of your products and, if you already have a shop, include links that lead to your Etsy account. By doing this, you will also get some feedback about your product or concept and you'll be able to gauge how good your idea sounds to others. A good seller should listen to feedback and values interactions with the customer.

Tips:

- Keep an eye out on which products gives you the biggest margin of profit and expand on that line.

- Try to become an expert on what you do. Remember that if you're good at creating something, then there are those who are already great at it. Keep honing and improving your craft so that you can grow and expand with the market.

- If you want to protect your creative product, then you can register your unique designs. All the information and registration forms needed to apply for copyright from the U.S. Copyright office can be found on the net from the government website.

Don't get discouraged when you find that the creations you love so much aren't really selling yet. Remember that you're no longer creating for yourself but for other people who might have different tastes than you personally. If you find that your creations aren't catching on, try making them in varied designs or colors and keep your target market in mind.

Check out the rest of this book on Amazon.com.

Other books written by me

(Check out these books on Amazon.com)

- **Penny Stocks:** *Investors Guide Made Simple – How to Find, Buy, Maximize Profits, and Minimize Losses with Penny Stock Trading*

- **FOREX Trading:** *A Simplified Guide To Maximizing Profits, Minimizing Losses and How to Use Fundamental Analysis & Trading Techniques to Thrive in a Bear and Bull Market*

- **Etsy:** *The Ultimate Guide Made Simple for Entrepreneurs to Start Their Handmade Business and Grow To an Etsy Empire*

www.ingramcontent.com/pod-product-compliance
Lightning Source LLC
Chambersburg PA
CBHW070406190526
45169CB00003B/1130